I dedicate this book to my son, Rocco.
Each and every day you inspire me to be the best version of myself.
Out of all the things in this world, being your mother is my favorite.
I love you always, Mama.

To learn more about this book and the author, visit
www.enlightenedmotherhood.com

THE RAINBOW TUNNEL

Written and illustrated by
Brittany Zancolli

Let's go on an adventure through the rainbow tunnel where you get to feel strong and confident!

You'll need to wiggle through each color, because the tunnel is small!
So, let's go!

On the count of three
say, "wiggle, wiggle, wiggle"
to get to the first color!

1..2..3..

WIGGLE, WIGGLE, WIGGLE!

Wow, you made it to the first color!

RED

and something is looking right at you...

It's an elephant!

The elephant says, "you are strong",
so you say it back, "I am strong".

Now you can wiggle to the next color!

1..2..3..

WIGGLE, WIGGLE, WIGGLE!

You made it to the color

ORANGE

and something is looking right at you...

It's a spider!!

The spider says, "you are creative",
so you say it back, "I am creative".

Now you can wiggle to the next color!

1..2..3..

WIGGLE, WIGGLE, WIGGLE!

You made it to the color

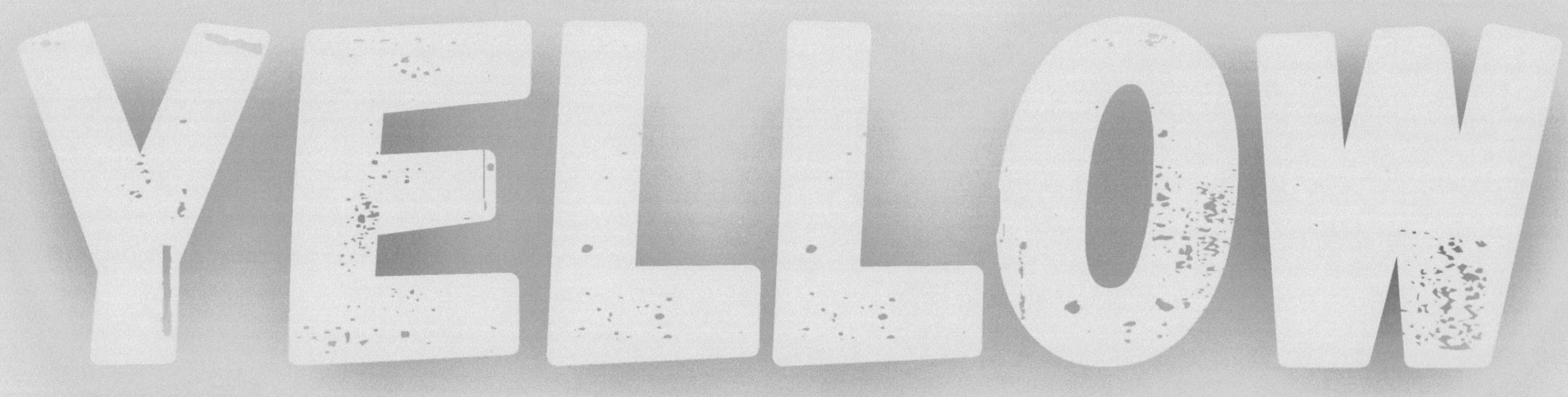

and something is looking right at you...

It's a lion!

The lion says, "you are confident",
so you say it back, "I am confident".

Now you can wiggle to the next color!

1..2..3..

WIGGLE, WIGGLE, WIGGLE!

You made it to the color

and something is looking right at you...

It's a butterfly!

The butterfly says, "you are kind",
so you say it back, "I am kind".

Now you can wiggle to the next color!

1..2..3..

WIGGLE, WIGGLE, WIGGLE!

You made it to the color

and something is looking right at you...

It's a wolf!

The wolf says, "you speak your truth",
so you say it back, "I speak my truth".

Now you can wiggle to the next color!

1..2..3..

WIGGLE, WIGGLE, WIGGLE!

You made it to the color

and something is looking right at you...

It's an owl!

The owl says, "you are enough",
so you say it back, "I am enough".

You had so much fun in all the colors of the rainbow
tunnel, and now it's time to wiggle your way out!

1..2..3..

WIGGLE, WIGGLE, WIGGLE!

You made it! You did such a good job wiggling through the rainbow tunnel, and now you feel the warmth of the sun all over your body!

The tunnel says "thank you!"

So you say it back "thank you!"

You look down to see all the colors of
the rainbow glowing on your body.
The colors of the rainbow will always
be apart of you.

The tunnel says
"All you ever need is within you".

So you say it back
"All I ever need is within me".